Anonymous

Thomas Hill Rich, a memorial

Anonymous

Thomas Hill Rich, a memorial

ISBN/EAN: 9783337732523

Printed in Europe, USA, Canada, Australia, Japan

Cover: Foto ©ninafisch / pixelio.de

More available books at **www.hansebooks.com**

THOMAS HILL RICH

A Memorial.

BY

CAROLINE W. D. RICH.

IDLEHAVEN.
1896.

TO THE NIECES OF

THOMAS HILL RICH,

Mrs. Peters, Mrs. Higgins, Mrs. Stupell,

THIS LITTLE BOOK

IS LOVINGLY DEDICATED.

*"And so the Word had breath and wrought
With human hands the creed of creeds
In loveliness of perfect deeds,
More strong than all poetic thought."*

Introduction.

In preparing this memorial there is no attempt to do more than to enshrine the memory of a modest man in this tangible form. It may be said of Professor Rich, truthfully, that his private character was of a rare order and his personal traits singularly lovable. It is not possible to give a correct impression to those who never met him. But those for whom this tribute is prepared will recognize the truth set forth in these pages. And if the brief outline of his life shall be helpful to any who are striving to find paths of usefulness, the object of this sketch will be accomplished.

The indefinable spirit of courtesy and gentle, high-bred personality of Professor Rich was nowhere so manifest as in the privacy of home. Never regarding his own ease—never forgetting the comfort of others—he was the one to whom each looked for aid, for comfort, for counsel. No visitor left his door without feeling the uplifting of his quiet influence. It was like a benediction. The sweetness and elegance of his manners gave him easy influence with those who came to him in their difficulties, enabling him to help, without wounding, even those who were in the wrong.

Professor Rich never talked much in general society except in an unobtrusive way. No one could have guessed the mass of information on all subjects which lay beneath that quiet exterior. Yet he was ever eager to learn, listening with close attention to others and replying with modesty.

One incident from many may illustrate this. In a company of clergymen, where a rather spirited talk was going on upon some Old Testament topic, they turned to him with the question: "Professor Rich, what do you think it means?" With a smile as modest as a child's, he replied: "I feel as though I know very little about it." This answer was so characteristic that all laughed heartily. He then gave his views, which were clear and conclusive, and were accepted by all present.

Professor Rich was cordially welcomed everywhere. But it was emphatically in the circle of his friends that his fascination was most apparent. It had the power of a strong character, all the more because the possessor was so unconscious of it. His daily and hourly life, his little acts, his pleasantries, were all as pure as if he was in the presence of God. In social gatherings he often left those whose company he enjoyed and sought those who felt ill at ease, to make for them a happier hour.

He did not talk much of himself; even his deepest griefs never got the better of his judgment, and his personal cares were kept sacredly in his own heart.

His life was always full of service for others. No personal gain could keep him from duty. He left his work when a teacher to be with his invalid mother, till she entered into her rest; for no one could serve her quite so much to her mind as this beloved son—her youngest born. And later he gave up his position again to render like service to his father, who needed such care for the only time in a long life. If need seemed to require it, he could do many things which *men* seldom attempt, perhaps having learned thus to be useful and helpful in many domestic ways during these long periods of ministry. The words of George Herbert came often to his lips when the necessary demands of the invalid were exhausting to mind and body:

"Who sweeps a room as for Thy laws
Makes that and the action fine."

The family pedigree was an honorable one, and he had a satisfaction in knowing it. But he never paraded the fact that his forefathers were connected with the Warwick blood on the father's side, though the record is unquestionable.

Thomas Hill Rich entered Bowdoin College, September, 1844, and was graduated from it in 1848. He entered Bangor Theological Seminary in 1849 and was graduated in 1852. It was this same year, it appears, that he received the degree of A.M. from his *Alma Mater*. He was elected assistant in the Hebrew immediately upon his graduation from the Seminary, and held this position for two years. Again, in 1866, he was invited to assist Dr. Talcott. He held this position till he came to Bates, September, 1872.

While living in Bangor he was elected deacon in the Third Parish Church, of which Rev. G. W. Field, D.D., was pastor and Mr. E. F. Duren, senior deacon.

Professor Rich came to Bates just when he was needed. He had a department to create; for the Divinity School had but recently been transferred from New Hampton, having small equipment and feeble existence, and the question was whether or not it could be continued. Only through the indomitable energy of that rare man—Professor Fullonton—did it then exist. There were few students and few teachers. Dr. Fullonton had been compelled by more pressing duties to give up the Hebrew. Indeed, in 1871 there was not one student for that department. The necessity for a knowledge of that language was not felt then, as now, by the Free Baptist denomination. The funds of the school were meagre; consequently the library was deficient in the literature of the Hebrew.

He felt these limitations keenly, having come from Bangor Seminary, where the Department of Sacred Literature stood out prominently under the masterful guidance of Dr. Talcott, with whom he had been so intimately associated. His ideals of what Hebrew should be to a clergyman had been strengthened by his close relations with such a scholar, and he ever referred to him as one who had led him into the beauties of a language which, later, had such attractions for him. In the spirit of utter unselfishness he set himself to work to interest those who were to preach the Christ "of whom Moses and the prophets did write." In this spirit he wrought till the end—at once an ideal teacher and a sincere Christian.

As a teacher his earnestness had a contagious quality, the more so because he never attempted to drive. He was ever a pupil with his pupils, ever learning while he led. He had genuine sympathy with those whom he instructed and unvarying courtesy toward them, as from a gentleman to gentlemen. It is possible that this unequipped department brought out the best qualities in him as teacher; for the very dearth of aid for the students from the library compelled him to draw freely from his own mental treasures. And his wide range of vision from the study of many languages now helped him to stand upon the heights and, like the Seer of old, point to the promised Messiah.

Apparently his absorption in others had left no room in his active brain to plan for his personal comfort, so that he came to Lewiston a single man. In the new atmosphere and new environments he felt the need of home ties as he had not while in his native city, where his sister—Mrs. Amos M. Roberts—had taken the mother-place to him after the parental home was no more.

At this distance he missed her loving thoughtfulness. In November, 1876, Professor Rich married and took up his residence in Auburn. Here some of his happiest years were spent. The High Street Congregational Church and its Sunday-school became his church home.

In the autumn of 1887 he built a modest house on Frye Street in Lewiston. This change of residence afforded him an opportunity to do more for his pupils, while it brought him into closer contact with the College and Divinity School Faculty, socially. Here he made pupils and associates welcome with that simple grace which was his pre-eminent characteristic.

As he had been when a student and among early friends, so he continued,—unflinching if duty demanded—self-sacrificing always. No one knew his struggles, his disappointments, his hopes, his burdens. Yet they surely came into his life experience, but he fought his battles alone.

In his scholarly instincts Professor Rich was critical, with intellectual humility so marked that it made him conservative. Yet he was singularly ready to accept the developments of science. Without egotism he decided for himself in his investigations, and what he knew was the result of most thorough and painstaking research.

He knew how to use books and make them reveal to him their stores. He did not collect a large library, but he had on his shelves the best—the rare and critical of all languages that could possibly aid him in his investigations.

FAMILY HISTORY.

Hosea Rich, M.D., was born in Charlton, Worcester County, Mass., October 1, 1780. He was son of Paul and Mary Rich, and grandson of Deacon Jonathan Dennis, who was a Representative for twenty successive years in the Massachusetts Legislature.

In his childhood he was inured to labor on the paternal farm, and thus by his physical training he laid the foundation of that vigorous constitution, that robust health, which continued to the late evening of life, so that he always possessed a sound mind in a sound body.

He early manifested a decided preference for the study of medicine, but as he was the only surviving son his parents desired to retain his services on the farm; yet by the advice of his grandfather they at last reluctantly yielded to his importunity, and after attending a common school and receiving instruction from a clergyman of his native town, he became a medical student of Dr. John Elliot Eaton, a skillful physician of Dudley, Mass., who was a graduate of Harvard University.

January 6, 1803, Dr. Rich married Mrs. Fanny Goodale, whose maiden name was Barker, and who died in May, 1864. By her he became the father of eight children, one of whom was an able physician, and the youngest of whom was the late Professor Thomas H. Rich.

In 1803, at the age of twenty-five, he began to seek a favorable location. He was induced by the late John Barker, Esq., a brother of Mrs. Rich, to establish himself in Bangor, Maine, where he arrived on July 4, 1805. There, for more than sixty years, he actively and successfully practiced medicine and surgery.

Dr. Rich was President of the Penobscot County Medical Association and of the Maine Medical Association. He received the honorary degree of M.D. from Bowdoin College in 1851.

At the time Dr. Rich began his professional career in Bangor he had a competitor in the person of Dr. Balch, who was a gentleman of popular manners and respectable professional skill, but with strong inclinations for political honors. Dr. Rich, on the other hand, had one object only in view, and that object was his profession. The result, as might be expected, was in every respect favorable. His science and reputation were ever advancing.

He loved the practice of medicine and also of surgery with an intensity unsurpassed. For this he sacrificed everything that stood in its way. Its duties to him were always paramount in importance, its emoluments subordinate. His services could always be commanded alike by the poor and the rich. No pestilence that walketh in darkness, no destruction that wasteth at noonday, neither summer's heat nor winter's cold, neither darkness nor distance, ever appalled or impeded him in the discharge of his beneficent work; but with him the path of duty was ever the path of pleasantness.

As a surgeon, he was cautious and conservative. Though fond of operating, he was more desirous to preserve than to amputate. His hand was firm and steady, without a tremor, to the last day of his life. He performed important operations very frequently, and was remarkably successful. His first capital operation was the amputation of a leg in 1809, and his last operation was the delicate one of couching for cataract, June 27, 1865, when at more than fourscore years, with natural force unabated, with clear eye and steady hand, he then gave the inestimable blessing of sight to a blind old man.

He was an universally popular man, and that is much to say. He saw nothing but his profession, and was constantly serving his fellowmen. He was very agreeable in his manners, and courteous to and honorable with all men. He was a very fine and impressive-looking man.

After his death, his life was briefly described and its merits and usefulness beautifully portrayed by the Rev. Dr. Charles C. Everett, then of the Unitarian pulpit in Bangor. Rev. Dr. Everett's allusions and descriptions were interesting and touching, and the following passage is quoted therefrom:

"One has gone from us whose usefulness is bound up with the history of our city almost from its beginning. For sixty years it has known no pause or rest. His usefulness was not the service of a slave or hireling, but it was the service of love. It was the outgrowth of an enthusiasm for the work he had chosen and of a genial and hearty interest in those about him. His profession was a life and not a livelihood. Rich and poor shared alike the blessing of its unselfish zeal. He accepted with a certain pride the most difficult and toilsome accompaniments of these great duties. All honored this simple and earnest life. All loved to see the venerable form, erect beneath the burden of years and of cares, pass through the streets on its errands of mercy. All took a certain pride in the hale and hearty age, and in the fine form of one whose life was thus identified with their own city."

JOHN A. PETERS.

Bangor, Me.

CONTRIBUTIONS.

The late Professor T. H. Rich of Cobb Divinity School I first knew intimately in a relation which proved revelatory. He was Professor of Hebrew, a ripe scholar, and a specialist in Holy Writ. I was a layman and a teacher of a Bible class at the High Street Congregational Church in Auburn. He declined my urgent request that he take my place, but he insisted on being my pupil. While, of course, I was delighted to have him in the class, his presence there seemed to me to be what it was in actuality, grotesque. But I think it was an excellent lesson to me in some of the benedictions of the Gospel. There was neither the affectation of humility nor the slightest conceit in Professor Rich. Some men have intellectual complacency when dispossessed of Phariseeism, but Professor Rich had neither of these traits. It goes without saying, if his Bible class teacher did not learn from such a pupil more than he could possibly impart to any of his pupils, that he was not only conspicuously unfit for instruction, but exceedingly disqualified from the teacher's first duty of learning.

First impressions of Professor Rich were fortified by a completer acquaintance. I must call him a personality quite unlike any I have ever met. Of course, we all like men to be themselves rather than echoes of others. The genuineness of Professor Rich was his felicity. To feminine delicacy and refinement, he united virile zeal in whatsoever he undertook. Whenever he read to me, as sometimes he did, with unobtrusive modesty, some of his versions from the Old Testament, I was impressed with the keen appreciation with which he saw the oriental life and mind. The rhythm of things was his inspiration. Words were pictures and music. He was an interlinear prophet. As a scholar and specialist I honor him for his fidelity to trifles as well as for his splendid intellectual horizon. His mind was not all latitude, not all longitude, but his mental and moral qualities were correlated in what tended to spherical completeness. I have seen so many specialists without breadth, so many inverted cones of wisdom, that Professor Rich's gifts of simplicity, catholicity, and modesty were to me a revelation of the sphere of breadth in which all inspiring life must start from the ground.

I cannot stay to enlarge on the felicities of Professor Rich's mind and heart, further than to add that they saturated and created his conduct. His thoughtfulness and consideration followed me. He was a friend to tie to, because he was loyal, charitable, and given to putting the best impressions on the acts of others as well as on Holy Writ. His mind and his heart were so pure that to caricature him would be much like caricaturing an orchard in June.

I was astonished on completer acquaintance to find that the Professor knew the art of enjoyment. He possessed a keen sense of humor. He could laugh from the bottom of his heart, rather than from the top of his head. The humanity of the Professor delighted me. He was what is better than likeable — he was lovable.

While away from home, a few years ago, I received occasional letters from him, which showed him to have been in the unconscious possession of a somewhat superseded art. His letters told just what one wished to know of the neighborhood with which we were both identified; told it gracefully and happily, in the delightful way of Charles Lamb rather than in the fragmentary way of the typewriter. His thoughtfulness was conspicuous in what he wrote as in what he did.

His death in the midst of usefulness makes it necessary to reconcile arrested careers here with implicit faith in immortal development yonder, if we would justify the power of God by His love.

FRANK L. DINGLEY.

Professor Rich was an admirable representative of true manhood. As a teacher his abilities were of the first quality. He left behind him only the sweetest influences. To few persons do the words apply as well:

"His life was gentle; and the elements
So mix'd in him, that Nature might stand up,
And say to all the world, *This was a man!*"

O. B. CHENEY.

On July 6, 1893, Professor Rich went out from his beautiful home to return in less than a quarter of an hour borne tenderly by those upon whom the awe of his sudden death had so swiftly descended. In the three years that have passed there have come from many and distant places messages of sympathy, tributes of love and reverence, that show how deep and wide was the influence of a life never withdrawn from the quiet paths of scholarship and the gentle ministrations of love.

Thomas Hill Rich was born in Bangor, September 5, 1822. His father, Hosea Rich, and his mother, Frances (Barker) Rich, were of English descent, and of ancestry so marked that their lineage is clearly traceable through many generations,—the father's through more than four centuries. Their youngest child inherited the distinctive traits of each parent. His father was for many years one of the foremost and best-known physicians in Maine. Coming in his early manhood with his wife from their home in Worcester County, Mass., he won a distinction in his profession that not only made him one of the leading citizens of Bangor, but an authority in surgery quoted in Europe as well as in America. The son inherited his father's thoroughness, persistency, and love of research, while to his mother he owed that gentleness, modesty, and constant thoughtfulness for others which impressed every one who knew him. From his mother, too, he received that constant encouragement to study and self-improvement which the absorbing duties of an active professional life forbade from his father. By her, also, were nurtured that reverence, humility, and helpfulness which made the piety of her son at once so beautiful and so practical. Converted while but a schoolboy, through all subsequent changes he carried the evidence of his discipleship in his life.

Preparing for college in the Bangor High School, he entered Bowdoin in 1844, and graduated in 1848. Of his scholarly spirit and his progress as a student it is unnecessary to speak. To his life in college a classmate pays this tribute:

"He was a real friend to every poor, sick,

and troubled boy in college. He was a friend to us all without any distinction of clubs or societies. I think he had the love and respect of every man in every class, . . . not only for his kindness in their sickness and trouble but for his manifest interest in their personal religious welfare. I think he made it a point to have a personal conversation on religious things with every student. I never met a more earnest and devoted Christian in all my life."

The value of this testimony can be appreciated only by those who knew Professor Rich. Never obtrusive, gifted with a delicate sense of what belongs to the rights of others, shrinking from controversy, and reading as by intuition the feelings of a companion before they could be expressed in words—he gave proof in these successful endeavors to touch the hearts and influence the lives of his fellow-students not merely of tactful sympathy but of a rare moral courage. Nor was this manifested in his college life alone. The casual observer might be impressed only by his gentleness and modesty. Those who enjoyed his friendship know how persistently true he was to his convictions. Few men have shown equal fidelity to high ideals. It would be difficult to conceive of his pure life as adjusting itself to the lower standards of the selfish and the superficial. His entire mode of life was a reflection of his own individuality. His was an exacting, though a healthy conscience, but he gave heed to it, whatever might seem to be the exigencies of the hour. No demands of social or political life could move this quiet man to violate his own sense of the right, the fitting.

He was always peculiarly tender toward the sick, often ministering to them with his own hands and always with a fine sense of the needs of the sufferer which made his very presence grateful and refreshing. Entering, in 1849, Bangor Theological Seminary, he graduated in 1852, and was at once appointed assistant instructor in Hebrew. Evidently the language that proved so fascinating to him through his later life had deeply interested him at his first acquaintance. Subsequently he taught some years in the Seminary at Bucksport, and afterward for a little less than two years in the Portland High School during the principalship of Dr. J. H. Hanson. Summoned from this position to minister again to an invalid in his father's home, he at length resumed the work of assistant instructor in Hebrew in the Theological Seminary, Bangor. Here he formed many precious and enduring friendships. The students were drawn to him not only by his helpfulness as a teacher but by the charm of a nature exquisitely refined and sympathetic. Keenly sensitive to the harsh and painful in human experience, he yet, following in the footsteps of his master, sought out the poor and neglected, and patiently and methodically devoted himself to supplying both their bodily and their spiritual needs. The interpretation which he thus gave of the missionary spirit and endeavor was quite as helpful to the young men in the Seminary as any exegesis could be, however searching and true. The direct testimony of one of the students of that period shows that the lesson thus practically given was not lost.

In 1872, the call to the professorship of Hebrew in the Theological Department of Bates College (now Cobb Divinity School) seemed to open a wider sphere of usefulness to Mr. Rich, and he left Bangor for Lewiston. There for twenty-one years he has been the beloved professor, delighting in his work and the companionships that it brought him. Untiring in his preparation for the recitation room and in his painstaking and thorough instruction, eagerly solicitous for the progress of every one of his students, he yet found time to interest himself in the social life of the school and the community. Even before he had provided for himself a home, he made his students familiar with the attractions of his tasteful rooms, becoming to them not only their honored teacher but their dear personal friend.

He shared their joys and their sorrows, comforted and helped them in their troubles, and steadily imparted to them the elevating and refining influence of his own pure tastes and scholarly spirit.

After his marriage in 1876, his home was the delightful resort of students, fellow-teachers, and friends. Always putting a very modest estimate upon his own attainments, he was eager to impart whatever of value he had.

"And gladly would he learn and gladly teach."

With a wife thoroughly in sympathy with his tastes, he succeeded in making his quiet and unpretentious home a place at once restful and beautiful to every visitor. Nothing gave him more pleasure than to entertain his friends, and he was one of the most successful of hosts. He studied to make his guests happy, but his attentions to them were as natural and artless as those of a child. In their society he indulged that love of pleasantry which his intimate friends know to have been so characteristic. He had both wit and humor, and they were always as pure and refined as they were spontaneous!

Happy is the man who never wholly ceases to be a boy! Few have in equal degree with Professor Rich retained through a long life that love of nature and that susceptibility to its influence which is justly considered so choice a part of one's endowment in youth. The sunrise and the sunset, the songs of the birds, and the silent beauty of the stars, never lost their charm for him. As he took from his window his favorite morning view, he would often exclaim, "It is more beautiful than ever before." From his first walk in spring to his last in autumn, he rarely returned to his home without bringing some leafy token of his rambles.

His perennial youth showed itself, too, in his love for children, and the ease with which he entered into their fancies and pleasures. They always loved him and were at home with him. He had a sincere respect for the individuality of each, however young, and won confidence by a sympathy which was instinctively felt to be genuine.

Equally interesting to him was the life of young men and young women. He appreciated the possibilities before them and was eager to be helpful to them.

A single example out of the many that his life afforded deserves notice. It is full of inspiration to all minds. A young man sixteen years of age went from northern Maine to work in the Journal office in Lewiston. Some of his friends wrote Professor Rich about him. After Professor Rich's death Mrs. Rich received a letter from this young man, now in business in a large city, in which, though an entire stranger to her, he expressed his sympathy and regret for her loss. I quote a few sentences: "He made it his business to befriend me. It was my privilege to attend church with him regularly, and on several occasions to take tea with him in his apartments. Having no father, I felt for him the affection of a son, and although a multiplicity of cares and troubles have since forced me to neglect him, I have never for one instant forgotten him, nor ever shall, as the kindest, most disinterested friend a young man could possibly have."

This letter gives the key-note to the character of Professor Rich. It was the Christian motive of disinterested helpfulness that ruled his life. He had the aspirations and attainments of a true scholar, but he lived to do good. His published works show how careful and finished was his scholarship, but they show even more impressively his earnest purpose to make God's word helpful to those who should read those portions of it that he had so carefully translated.

He was a member of the American Oriental Society and one of the first members of the Society of Biblical Literature and Exegesis. He was also a member of the Genealogical Society of Maine and of the Maine Historical Society. His contributions to religious periodicals were numerous and highly prized. At Professor Harper's personal request he had contributed articles to "The Old and New Testament Student." He had also written for the "Treasury," and was by special request to furnish another article to appear in the early fall. His four published works have established his reputation as a Hebrew scholar. But an honest expression of thanks for the help that he had given toward the better understanding of some passage of scripture was worth more to him than the amplest tribute to his scholarship.

Such expressions often came to him, and they always gave him new joy in his work. In his translations, the peculiar qualities of his style appear to the best advantage—above all his fine choice of words. He conscientiously strove to reproduce, as far as possible, the exact thought of the original. To this end he compared not only the Arabic and Syriac versions of the Old Testament, not only the Septuagint and the Vulgate, but the translations into French and German, seeking to find through the careful study of all some means of conveying the thought more precisely.

Incidental reference has been made to his favorite studies. He was not unfamiliar with Spanish and Italian. He was a constant reader not only of French and German works, but of the English classics. Of Shakespeare and Milton he was always an appreciative student.

Yet few scholars have conceded so much to the diversions of life. Every day found him for a little while at the piano; in the morning and on Sundays singing his favorite hymns, at other times renewing the past with long familiar songs. His love of melody manifested itself, too, in his writings. They were characterized not only by choice diction, simplicity, and directness, but by their fine rhythmical effect. His exquisite ear for cadences and musical balances was, doubtless, in part the result of his loving study of Hebrew parallelisms.

To his life-long study of Hebrew, too, is referable in some degree the rich quaintness of his style, especially in his translations. This quality was in part, also, the result of his deep interest in his mother tongue. For his use of English reflected in a pleasing way the etymology of his carefully chosen words. Language to him was fragrant with associations—the words suggesting their primitive meanings and their use by his favorite authors. Of this habit of his mind, his best-known lecture, "Lessons in Words," was one of the natural fruits. The revision of this lecture and of his recent translation of Habakkuk occupied nearly all of his last day on earth. It was Thursday, and on the next Sunday evening he was to read the translation at the Congregational church in Kennebunkport. On August 12th he was to give the lecture in the Chautauqua Assembly course at Fryeburg; and in the same place on August 15th, he was again to present his translation in a Bible reading. For three hours he had sat in his study, the soft tones of his voice just audible in the adjoining room, as, after his custom, he slowly read each sentence, testing its flow and cadence. About half-past four o'clock in the afternoon he rose, saying cheerily to his wife, "I am going now," words whose deep significance was sadly disclosed only a few minutes later.

What wonder that such a man had friends! Through his entire life, to old and young, to rich and poor, to the learned and the unlettered, he had "shown himself friendly." Peculiarly tender were his feelings toward his own kindred. For his early home-friends and his relatives, time could only deepen and strengthen his affectionate regard. He appreciated their thoughtfulness for him. Devoted to his books, he felt himself peculiarly favored in being able to have in his business affairs such faithful and capable counselors. To Chief Justice Peters, the husband of one of his nieces, he felt himself, as the writer has often heard him say, under signal obligations for his constant and disinterested assistance in affairs of great importance. Nor was any of the many favors done him by his numerous friends ever forgotten. He had a large correspondence, for he made new friends at every period of his life, and a friendship once formed was forever sacred to him. His sudden removal from the old familiar friends and places abruptly terminated this intercourse by letters after it had been maintained in some instances for more than two-score years.

It is now three years since the life of our friend was withdrawn from the quiet associations with which it so harmoniously blended. His was an individuality never accentuated by ambition, seldom agitated by marked changes in plans or experience. Yet it is distinctly outlined in the minds of all who had felt its gracious influence. Form, face, expression, voice, and movement seemed perfectly responsive to the living soul. And to-day Professor Rich is to those who really knew him a sacred presence rather than a cherished memory. The most life-like photograph, the most speaking portrait, could scarcely more than confirm the abiding sense of his serene and steadfast personality. Thus "he being dead yet speaketh."

GEORGE C. CHASE.

President of Bates College, Lewiston, Me.

NEW HAVEN, CONN., April 23, 1896.

Dear Mrs. Rich:

I am glad you are to prepare a memorial of your husband. I knew him intimately when I resided in Bangor. I esteemed him as a man of superior intellect and scholarship and of very lovely character. I thought him admirably fitted for the professorship which he held, and was glad when I heard he had accepted it and had begun his work on a line so well suited to his taste and for which he was so well fitted. The volumes which he published were carefully prepared, evinced thorough scholarship, and were fitted to be instructive and helpful to the reader. He was a very estimable man, and I heartily sympathize with you in your sorrowful bereavement.

With cordial regard,

Very truly yours,

SAMUEL HARRIS.

I cannot forbear expressing my great sorrow for his death, both as the loss to me of a much esteemed friend and the loss to the church of a highly esteemed and influential scholar and teacher. . . . He was a man of lovely spirit. He was like Paul, who says, "We were gentle among you," and a beautiful example of conformity with the repeated apostolic requirement, "Be gentle toward all men." He was also a man of fine intellect and of high scholarship in his department. He is a great loss to all.

S. H.——.

(Extract from a letter, July, 1893.)

I count it a privilege to have my name enrolled among the friends of Thomas H. Rich. My acquaintance with him began as long ago as 1859, and there must be very few persons living who have known him so long and so intimately as a companion, fellow-student, guest, and correspondent. He was always a welcome visitor at my house, where his interest in children and young people found kindly expression, perhaps in a dish of "honey candy" which he had himself compounded with womanly skill and personal satisfaction, or in the gift of flowers which he had plucked from his father's garden, or in the offer of a drive over the Bangor hills.

For a number of years we had a weekly appointment for common reading, in English or Greek or German, which gave me ample opportunity to see how thoroughly he was accustomed to investigate every linguistic question and to base his conclusions on careful research. He lacked self-assertion, possibly, and was modest to a fault, but he knew that certainty must come from personal investigation, and so he would not shrink from any detail, but work out his conclusions by the use of all the means at his command. Accurate in his scholarship, painstaking in his search for truth, even when distrustful of his own ability, he set an example of conscientious fidelity to duty which every student may well follow.

In character he might fitly be described, like Nathaniel of old, as "an Israelite indeed in whom is no guile," for I never knew a man whose life was so thoroughly transparent. No Roentgen rays could have disclosed any subterfuge or crookedness in him.

His sweet disposition, his gentle manner, his soft, sweet voice, and his kindly, genuine sympathy with all who were in any manner of trouble, gave him special fitness for the office of a deacon, and for ministrations to the sick and needy. No rude questioning, no impatient complaint, no harsh utterance ever fell from his lips, and if his speech ever hesitated, perhaps his look and actions were more expressive of tender sympathy than a multitude of words could have been.

He must have shown the same characteristics in the professor's chair, bearing patiently the imperfections of his pupils, and setting them an example of unwearied and faithful study. In later years he often spoke to me in his letters of certain students in whose welfare and proficiency he was taking the deepest interest, and of whose success as ministers of the Word he felt confident. Of these there must be not a few who revere his memory and recall his work for them with unbounded satisfaction.

His occasional publications are characteristic of the man, illustrating his habit of elaborating details, his nice discriminations, his exquisite taste. His was the quiet, uneventful life of the scholar, seeking wisdom for its own sake and that he might impart it to others, and thus enjoying equally the acquisition and the imparting, and the assurance at the same time that he was serving God in his generation and according to the measure of his ability.

I honor his memory and gladly join with others in offering this brief and imperfect tribute.

EDWARD W. GILMAN.

Bible House, New York.

Every mention of his name carries my mind back to times more than thirty years ago, and our friendship then formed became intimacy of the closest kind, with frequent stated meetings for reading and study.

. . . .

He was distrustful of himself in those days, but what he knew, he knew; and his careful habits of study were preparing the way for research and confident conclusions such as are shown in his publications of late years.

In our family, also, he made himself at home; fond of the children as they were of him, and glad to make them happy by any means in his power. He was not a man to let go any friendship which he had taken up—a fact which was evinced by the interest with which he followed the career of students or others whom he had taught or befriended.

. . . .

I have before me his photograph, endorsed with his own name, with the date of November 11, 1892, which reproduces finely the outline of his face and the eagerness of his gaze from beneath his overhanging eyebrows.

Sincerely yours,
E. W. G.

(Extract from letter of 1893.)

BANGOR, June 13, 1896.

My Dear Mrs. Rich:

I have thought of Deacon Rich while living among us as one who in an unusual degree was filled with the Holy Spirit; who sat at the feet of Jesus, and learned of Him; who lived above the world while living in it, having the simplicity that was in Christ, desiring the sincere milk of the Word that he might grow thereby. He heard the Shepherd's voice, and followed Him. His was the humble and contrite spirit with which God dwells, whose communion and fellowship is with the Father and with His Son Jesus Christ. He gave evidence that "to be spiritually minded is life and peace." It might be said of him, "Thy gentleness hath made me great."

His life and work, permeated by such characteristics, was sweet, uplifting, and ennobling. He manifested love and good-will to all, seeking opportunities to minister to the poor and needy, the suffering and bereaved. We were drawn near to God by his prayers, and strengthened by his words concerning Christ and the things pertaining to His kingdom.

He took great delight in the study of God's word; it was his meditation day and night; and in after life by unfolding its treasures he aided much those who came under his influence and instruction.

The following words of Robert W. Barbour seem applicable to him:

"The ornament of a meek and quiet spirit is like the dust from flowers in bloom. It insinuates and distills. The meek man is not without opinions, or a stranger to enterprise; but he has no desire to see his opinions imposed on others. Children find out the meek, for meekness is the childhood of the soul. Haughty men are never young, and the meek never grow old."

He walked with God, and was not, for God took him. What must be his joy now, in continuing his service in the heavenly life, in knowing even as he is known, in seeing face to face Him whom not having seen he loved here below.

Yours very truly,

E. F. DUREN.

Bangor, 1896.

My classmate Rich's influence in his college life was that of an unobtrusive though not silent and courage-lacking man. Subjectively his religion was a love of the right and of goodness and truth with sincerity, consistency, firmness, and modesty; objectively it was right-doing toward all, without selfishness, and with that charity which the apostle declares to be greater than faith or hope. That outflow of kindly sympathy which led him in his native city to seek out the poor in their homes, and under the cover of darkness to carry succor to the widow and the orphan, in college led him to seek the acquaintance of entering boys whom he had reason to suppose might feel deeply the separation from home or be exposed to rough experiences or seductive temptations, and render the comfort of his cheer or perhaps the actual shelter of his protection—for he was never afraid to face his fellow-students when they were in the wrong. In case of sickness, too, I do not believe that the room of a fellow-student was ever wanting of his kind and helpful visits.

This was his Christian character in college from the day of his entrance to the day of his graduation, seen and known of all. What impression it made no one can tell, but it cannot be that it was not a real and lasting one in its silent action. J. B. SEWALL.

Dear Mrs. Rich:

If we can give our friends pleasure here on earth, perhaps we can give them pleasure in heaven. They may think of us oftener than we do of them. They may know of us more than we do of them. In the midst of their joys there may be room for many a tender thought of our little life here below—the life they once lived, woven out of the same joys and sorrows, the same hopes, ambitions, endeavors. And when we try, even in our poor way, to make sacred and permanent all that was sweet and holy in their memory here on earth, it must add a fresh thrill of pleasure to their hearts even in heaven.

I first met your husband in college. He was a member of the Senior Class, and I had just entered as a Sophomore. To me, the distance between was quite immeasurable. A Senior was a man of dignity and erudition; a man of affairs; a man of the world; while a Sophomore was still in his callow youth, and had no particular rights that an upper-classman was bound to respect. It was a surprise to me, therefore, when he bridged the gulf, and by his numberless acts of kindness and consideration fastened my friendship to him for life. To be sure a sordid mind might suggest that he was simply "fishing" me—fishing me for the A Δ on the one hand, and the Praying Circle on the other. He was a member of both, and into both I followed him in due time. But the same kindly attentions, the same thoughtful and almost paternal care, continued long after that; and no one could imagine that such persistent friendliness could come from any other motive than the genuine Christian nature of the man.

For some years I was out of the country and lost sight of him. But after my return I found he had quietly settled himself down in the teacher's chair—the one pursuit of all others for which his abilities and tastes were evidently foreordained. In that profession he spent his life. Of his success those who have enjoyed his instructions can testify. His published translations from the Hebrew bear witness to his scholarship and his scrupulous fidelity; and show with what sympathy and insight he entered into the visions of the ancient seer. Their metrical form exhibits much of the poetic fire and spiritual energy of the original. His work as an interpreter of the Old Testament scriptures was not simply linguistic and exegetical, but also literary and spiritual.

He was a man of excessive modesty, of quiet refinement and feminine delicacy. He had no taste for notoriety. Life pleased him best when it was spent

Far from the madding crowd's ignoble strife,

in the quiet joys of the fireside, or in the seclusion of his library. His beloved books were personal friends; and in the daily routine of class work his mind and heart were continually refreshed by their companionship. His intellectual nature was satisfied and inspired by the high themes which formed the subject-matter of his daily study. And underneath all stood the solid foundation of his Christian manhood, a profound conviction of the ever-present sovereign of his heart, the Lord Jesus Christ, and an ardent faith in the great verities of the unseen world. We can well imagine that his sudden translation from the earthly work to the heavenly found him well prepared by faith, and discipline, and study, to enter upon new and larger methods of serving his Master. And the same powers which were so fully enlisted here, now expanded and hallowed and purified, we can think of as still more happily engaged in loftier service of his Lord, and in personal fellowship with the prophets and sages whose wisdom it was his delight to study here below. Very sincerely yours,

JOHN S. SEWALL.

Bangor Theological Seminary.

BUCKSPORT, ME.

Dear Mrs. Rich:

What your loss is I think I can better understand than most, knowing Professor Rich so well. As I recall those Seminary days of study, and later on when, broken down in health, I had returned to my old home,* his frequent little calls and visits, I seem to see his loving face and hear his gentle voice and receive the benediction of his presence. He was a loving friend, a constant friend, a faithful friend. Not many such are found. Earth is a sweeter place while they tarry here below, and departing, heaven becomes more winsome and attractive.

But he has gone; but going has left for you the Past, with all your mutual achievements and enjoyments; the Present, with all its sweet recollections and blessed anticipations; the Future, with its glorious realizations and blissful reunions. Not many in their hour of sorest loss have left so many sources of highest comfort. ALFRED L. SKINNER.

I first met Mr. Rich in college. I was late about joining my class, was blue and homesick. His kind words and acts cheered me up and inspired me with a love and respect for him which has never known any interruption from that day to this. And not only to me was he a real friend, but to every poor, sick, or troubled boy in college. He was a friend to us all

---

* Professor Rich was then teaching in the seminary in Bucksport.

without any distinction of clubs or societies. I think he had the love and respect of every man in every class. They loved and respected him not only for his kindness in their sickness and troubles, but for his manifested interest in their personal religious welfare. I think he made it a point to have a personal conversation on their personal interest in religious things with every student. I have never met a more earnest and devoted Christian in all my life.

One incident in his college life I have thought of a thousand times as evidence of this self-sacrificing nature. It was his taking under his sheltering wing a boy of another class, much younger than himself, who had fallen into the hands of evil associates and consequent evil habits. He even took him to be his roommate for a time, uncongenial as he must have been. It was always a mystery to me how he got him there, such was the great difference of their characters and habits. But he did it, and kept him there and brought him back to sobriety and made him a useful man, who became prominent in his profession in Washington.

It has been a great pleasure to me to think that I ever became acquainted with him and could number him among my friends.

G. S. NEWCOMB.

Westboro, Mass.

BURLINGTON, VT., July 9, 1896.

Dear Mrs. Rich:

Strange as it may seem to you, your letter is the first intimation I have had of the death of my excellent college mate, Prof. Thomas H. Rich.

His example probably influenced me more than that of any other student. I was but fifteen, and he, whatever was his age, was already remarkably mature in character and conduct. I sat at the same table with him during my first term at Bowdoin, and I can see him before me as I write. He was in the middle, a sort of president of the mess. I sat at the end toward the east. His handsome face became almost brilliant as soon as he entered into conversation with other students. Boy as I was, he treated me with marked respect, listened carefully to what I said, and though he might differ from me, his courtesy removed all the sting of opposition. Everybody said, whether they liked Rich or not, "He is a sincere Christian." In fact, he always appeared to me more like a father than a companion, and I would rather have enjoyed breaking him up, having an occasional fisticuff or wrestle; but I never could effect that naughty object with Rich. His gentleness, his sweetness, his sincerity, his charming manners, all combined to produce upon those who came in contact with him an ineffaceable impression of the strength of a chastened Christian spirit. His firmness, his manliness, his courage, his fortitude, and his persistent energy were as remarkable as his gentle nature; and had he taken the warlike turn, I doubt if Joshua of old would not have been equaled by him in the leading of men and in the commanding of armies.

I have not been acquainted with the work of Mr. Rich's later years, but shall be happy indeed to see how those who are intimate with him all along, show the developments of time.

Yes, you say truly, "the light has gone up higher," but its remembrance is still bright before my vision, though it is fifty years since it helped to lighten my path and brighten my environment.

May the Lord comfort and bless you, whose life privileges have been so pleasant and so great in his companionship.

Sincerely yours,
OLIVER OTIS HOWARD.

President H. Q. Butterfield of Olivet College wrote of Professor Rich in 1893, on learning of his death:

Dear Mrs. Rich:
Your husband and I were born the same year, and he was just a month younger than I. . . . . He was one class in advance of me in Bangor Seminary. Though we were graduated at College the same year, our associations in the Seminary were not so intimate as those of classmates. Yet I knew him well and respected him highly. Though we met but infrequently, yet I have for years had in memory the outline of his character — the frame-work of that finished picture which your letter and Professor Chase's have so exquisitely painted.

He was one, daily intercourse with whom would have been a daily delight to me. You are fortunate in having been the wife of such a man. The majority of husbands are not cast in a mold so fine. For a time you are to hear his musical voice only in memory; but you are as sure to hear its real tones again as you are to hear the voice of Him who is the Resurrection and the Life. That wealth of Biblical learning has not perished. The ship has not been broken where two seas meet and the lading cast into the deep. The gathered treasures of his life are capital with which to begin business in the life eternal. The knowledge and wisdom stored in College and Seminary are due preparation for the heavenly university. . . . I doubt not your husband will still delight in his Hebrew.

To know him a little was to know him much,—for such was the simplicity of his character and the unobtrusive constancy of his ministry in the world, the whole reality of his life seemed to find expression at every contact one was privileged to have with him, brief and incidental as it might be. . . . . We shall not look upon his like again. So far as I know, the world does not hold another man whose qualities, make-up, and personal unity in any considerable degree resemble Professor Rich. As he was a peculiar gift of God, so I believe his vocation and ministry have found peculiar honor in the Kingdom of God. . . . . C.
Portland.

He was one of my first friends in Bowdoin College, though he was a Senior when I entered—Sophomore. The fact of my loneliness . . . . . drew out his sympathies and he was very kind and helpful to me. . . . . Our acquaintance soon ripened into friendship, and that friendship has continued ever since. . . . . . He was always a scholar,—a man of scrupulous fidelity in all his work, and of tender and kindly temper toward all around him. I have always esteemed him as a man of sincere and elevated piety, and that serene inner life showed itself outwardly in a consistent and conscientious walk before the world. . . . The sudden transfer from the earthly to the heavenly must have been to him such a glorious surprise—so magnificent, so blessed, so infinitely better than anything his imagination had ever dreamed!

Tacoma, Wash.
(Extract from letter.)

From Rev. Henry Blodgett,
Formerly Missionary in Pekin, China.

. . . . .

I never knew a purer soul—a more blameless soul, one who walked more closely with the Lord, who was more careful to keep a conscience void of offence toward God and toward man, one who had so great simplicity of heart and life, and who was so truly and entirely humble. My acquaintance with Mr. Rich commenced in Bangor Theological Seminary. I can never forget his bathing my head all night long with most loving care, at a time when I had a sharp attack of illness.

It was only during a part of one year that we were associated in the Seminary at Bangor, he having entered the Class of '49, while I left during the year 1850.

In the Seminary, his singularly modest, diffident, and retiring disposition, combined with his careful and accurate scholarship, his simple and child-like piety, won for him the respect and affection of all. . . . .

In 1853 he taught in the East Maine Conference Seminary at Bucksport, Me., and roomed in the sightly hall which crowned the summit of Oak Hill. There I called upon him in his lovely retreat. He was cheerful and contented, and very much beloved by his pupils. "You would think," said he, "that the students would not obey me, that I could not maintain discipline in my classes. But in some way, I cannot tell how it is, at the least tap of my pencil upon the table they instantly give heed to my wishes."

When I next met him he was Professor of Hebrew in the Theological Seminary in Lewiston, Maine. The same qualities of diligent, conscientious scholarship, combined with his loving Christian character, greatly endeared him to his pupils here. He had found his home and his work. His classes loved and revered him. He had become united in marriage with one of congenial tastes and sympathies, and his daily life flowed on in a tranquil stream in love to God and service to his fellow-men. . . . .

. . . . . There was in him a certain unworldliness of mind, and yet he gave careful attention to every duty. Pellucid in character and motives, he shrank from every approach of evil. His was a hidden life—"Hid with Christ in God."

A book-mark lies in my Bible made in early years by his own handiwork. The motto inscribed upon it is, "No Cross on Earth, no Crown in Heaven." By this motto he lived. Yet his life was joyous, serene, and full of hope.

One might say that an unloving word or a harsh criticism, whether spoken to or concerning another, never escaped his lips. The law of kindness was in his speech and deeds of kindness were wrought by his hands. In early life he had nursed a brother (with whose religious sentiments he had no sympathy) with unwearied fidelity and tenderness through a protracted and painful illness, terminating fatally. Students and pupils shared the same watchful care. . . . The savor of his godly life remains and will remain in the hearts of all who knew him.

. . . .

HENRY BLODGETT.

I cannot claim to have had intimacy of friendship with Professor Rich, and our different lines of study did not enable me to appreciate at their true value his attainments in his own chosen field of labor. No one, however, could be admitted even to the outer circle of his friends without being impressed by the rare sweetness and unselfishness and spirituality of his nature; and no one could be, even for a little while, his pupil without recognizing the genuineness of his patient and thorough scholarship.

As a student in Bangor Theological Seminary I first came to know his patience and thoroughness as a teacher, and those qualities were always associated in my mind with the gentleness and courtesy of his intercourse, and the evident sincerity of his friendship. It was in Bangor, too, that I first saw and honored the breadth of his sympathy and generosity toward the poor and unfortunate. He gave freely of his means to relieve their wants and to alleviate their sufferings; but, what was better than that, he gave no less freely of *himself*, of his warm sympathy, his personal ministrations, and his faith, to comfort and encourage them.

He always seemed to me the most modest and unassuming of men, and yet he never shrank from what came to him as the call of duty, or from what promised him the opportunity of helpfulness to others. His face was the sufficient pledge of the tenderness and purity of his heart, and what his face promised his heart and his hands were swift to fulfill.

His modesty seemed to prevent him from publishing much of the results of his study and insight into the treasures of the Old Testament scriptures, but the few things that he published were ample evidence of the exactness of his learning, the carefulness of his methods, and the independence of his interpretation.

The memory of his gentle and unselfish and consecrated life must be dear alike to his pupils and his friends, and an inspiration to similar unselfishness and consecration.

HENRY L. CHAPMAN.
Brunswick, Me.

FROM CALIFORNIA.

. . . We were school-mates in the Bangor High School, preparing for college, and we had a boys' prayer-meeting of which he was the leader. . . . . He has had a warm place in my memory ever since those college days. He studied the classics with patient enthusiasm, a precursor of what he achieved in later years. He would work over a translation—polish it, perfect it—till he came fully to apprehend what translation meant, and could do that work confidently and effectively. It was interesting in Seminary days to see how what he acquired thus in College was brought to bear on his study of God's word. His enthusiasm grew. The new light on what was to him the dearest and best of all books rewarded him abundantly for all the toil of previous years.

(Extract from letter of 1893.)

. . . . . .

We shall never forget those who have gone from our own homes and hearts, and we always love to review their lives. But with the many, they pass out of a living interest. I was always struck by Professor Rich's disinterested thoughtfulness. His special ministrations seemed to grow out of his great tenderness for an invalid mother, and began even in his boyhood; and after she needed his care no longer, he seemed to be ever on the lookout for some opportunity to minister. He did not wait to hear about the needy ones; he sought them out. He found a poor lame boy . . . who was unable to walk; and for him he procured a chair, which enabled him to roll himself about. A lame deformed girl was clothed almost by his benefactions; and to all the sick and lonely on the "Hill" he was bringing, ever, something nice to read or some new diversion. I used to be reminded sometimes, by his great desire to serve in the "ministry of love," of some of Alice Cary's lines:

Make me within the universal chain a link, whereby
There shall have been accomplished some slight gain
For men and women when I come to die.

My acquaintance with Professor Rich began away back in our teens, when we were both in Bangor High School. Many a time the way through Cicero and the Greek was smoothed by his patient helpfulness. He was both a classmate and room-mate of my brother William in Bowdoin, and was often at our house, and my mother was made very comfortable by his assurance that he would care for and comfort the little fellow . . . and I know he kept his promise well.

. . . .

I feel very familiar with those strong and beautiful characteristics which Professor Chase gave of him, and I could tell you by the hour how his thoughtful kindness beguiled many of my blind mother's dark hours. Many mornings of his busy student life he freely gave to her, reading to her aloud, often translating from the German some gem which he thought she would appreciate.

. . . .

His tasteful rooms, his warm heart, and ready purse were always free for any child of sorrow or want, whatever their trouble might be. Poor students—students with families or in times of sickness, felt him a friend in need.

. . . .

Yours affectionately,

Belfast.   E. M. POND.

. . . . I had the most profound respect for his delicate, artistic nature, his pure life, his serene and affectionate disposition, and, in fact, for the entire personality which made him one by himself. It might be said of him during his whole life that "like a fragrance from beyond the Gates," his influence filled and enriched "every life which approached it."

Of all men he seemed to me nearest perfection of any I have seen, ... the friend and companion of my early youth—my school friend.   P.

Derry, N. H.

Many young men have been influenced by him for good in their studies of the old Hebrew language. He was a great help to me in my years of student life. Much of my love for the languages came through him. . . . . . In the hours of sickness of our family he was a present help. . . . . .   EMERICH.

. . . . Now that he is dead I can only recall his kindness to me and the transparent whiteness of his love—the unassailable integrity of his character and the thoroughness of his scholarship. Professor Rich was among my earliest and warmest friends, and understood my work and motives where others were blindly ignorant. He gave me great encouragement by word and deed, and his simple, manly, consecrated life, joined with an uplifting faith, opened my eyes to behold afresh the "beauty of holiness in Christian character."

R.

Your honored and beloved husband I knew but little, save as he was known and read of all men. He was but nine years old when I entered college. . . . Years after I used to see him occasionally at Mrs. Crosby's . . . and a few times at Lewiston. But his face and his life were "easy reading." His tranquility and sweet modesty, his gentleness, his loving heart and enthusiastic scholarship, and love of good men and good things, that went with these, how manifest they were.

Rev. A. C. A.

1893.

From a Student.

The kindness of Professor Rich to me cannot be forgotten. His patience with and interest in each student that came under his care were manifest to all. In him the students of Cobb Divinity School lose a faithful friend and painstaking instructor, and heaven is richer by the advent of so sweet a spirit.

N. K. S.

Professor Rich breathed a fine atmosphere. I have seen him attempt to drive a nail, with sad disaster to thumb and fingers. He had little aptitude and small love for the mere mechanics of living. And yet with what rare skill could he, in friendly rivalry with the housekeeper, concoct "pop-overs" for a social tea or prepare a more delicate morsel to tempt an invalid appetite.

Gentleness, sympathy, tact, were his prevailing characteristics. They marked him everywhere. Making friendships was not a pastime with him. One admitted to his friendship entered into a sacred relation. His soul clave to his friend. If the friend was busy, Professor Rich was considerate, never forgetful. Continents and seas might intervene, yet the genial flow of loving thought and epistolary confidences irrigated the friend's life. He remembered his friend's anniversaries, his friend's experiences, his friend's foibles. He did not insist that his friend should conform to *his* ways. He took the friend as he was, and adapted himself to the friend. His self-sacrificing gentleness reminds me of Monseigneur Bienvenu, the good Bishop of D. in "Les Misérables."

As he was loving, sympathetic, and tactful with his friends, so was he with Language. Language was his friend. He loved Language. He studied her moods, yielded himself to her foibles, laid bare his soul to her secrets;—he courted her like a lover. Who will forget his chaste and loving homage to her in his lecture on "Words?" With what faithful solicitude he translated her subtle fancies from one tongue into another! Though he spoke English and taught Hebrew, he was familiar with French and German and Latin and Greek, and was more than acquainted with Spanish and Italian. For his paraphrases of the Psalms he was wont to search for weeks to find the fitting phrase to express an idea, taking into account sound, sense, etymology, and association. Fine distinctions and scholarly discriminations are found in his lines.

In conversation a ready *jeu d'esprit* marked his thought. No pun was ever a barbarism on his lips; it was a work of art. Language, as he used it, brought light; it was sunny. Simple and direct, it had the air of not going deeply, but it illumined, it gladdened, it inspired.

As an instructor Professor Rich became more enthusiastic, as time passed. "I am better able to teach," he said with each succeeding year. Not much ground, but all thoroughly, sympathetically, tactfully, he covered; that was his method. He did not follow ruts. He did not cling to old text-books, or bring antiquated, dog-eared manuscripts before his classes. So ardent was his love for Language that he studied her moods anew each morning and communed with her afresh each evening. Some new discovery, some small addition, always aroused his zeal, answered to his ambition, and enriched his work.

In rare earnestness and devotion did he perform all his tasks as a Christian scholar.

ALFRED WILLIAMS ANTHONY.
Cobb Divinity School.

FROM REV. R. M. COLE.

"The righteous shall be in everlasting remembrance." Professor Rich, of Cobb Divinity School in Lewiston, belonged to this class most assuredly, as all who knew him most unhesitatingly testify. The writer came into acquaintance with him in Bangor Seminary during the spring of 1867. He was assisting Dr. Talcott in teaching the Hebrew (he was a native of Bangor); and . . . in a quiet, unassuming way, did not a little to comfort the poor, the infirm, the unfortunate, and aged of the place.

I shall not soon forget the long walk we took together over west of the seminary, out into the suburbs, where he introduced me to one of his *protégés*, a poor hunchback girl in her teens. It was a very destitute family, as all the environments went to show. . . . . If he helped them in charitable ways, he also tried to furnish wood-sawing to the father, or other work to the mother, so they might work out a livelihood, and not become parasites on charity.

As an elder brother, but with a sympathy and interest as keen as a woman's, he was helpful to many a student, very considerately making such suggestions from time to time as would be of advantage to them in the future.

He arranged for meetings here and there in town, often taking along some of us students to speak. At other times we were invited to accompany him to relieve the monotony of life's declining years (in some suburban home).

He took much interest in sending out the

"boys" for their future work, especially those who went far hence to the Gentiles.

Not a few choice keepsakes would he put into their hands, backing them up with his blessing and prayers, together with pledges of epistolary remembrance. For years he gave us the comfort of his full, familiar letters. The last time I met the good man was in 1875, and he surprised me by a brief visit among the granite hills of my native State, while we were in the country. Previous to this visit from him he had invited and paid the expenses of the missionary, on from Boston to his own home in Lewiston.

Bitlis, Kourdistan, Turkey in Asia.

. . . . . .

How gentle and true he always was! And what a radiant benediction his presence always left upon one's mind!

I have never known just such a rare combination of gentle courtesy and transparent genuineness of character, with such real scholarly strength.

. . . . . .

F. E. CLARK,
President of United Society of Christian Endeavor.

. . . .

Professor Rich was one of our oldest and best-beloved friends, and although we had not seen him for so many years, the world was brighter to us in the knowledge of his life and work. . . . . . .

Dresden, Germany.

. . . .
. . . . . .

He lived a life so beautiful, so rounded in completeness; he was so happy in doing his Master's work on earth! I think of him in the "house beautiful" with the dear ones gone on before. . . . .

. . . . The encouraging word, the gentle courtliness of his presence, the pure spirit of thought and deed, fall upon me, even now, like a benediction.

In his last visit to me (I was ill at the time) he said, when leaving, "The dear Father knows all our pain and sorrow; lean hard upon Him; He will sustain and comfort you."

. . . . . .

G. W.

A gentle spirit; a nature fluent yet of good substance, like mercury; capable of spiritual affinities chemical in their intimacy, and none the less indissoluble because free from violence in the making; a man of so single a mind that when he was once understood one could never have any doubts about him; a wholesome influence in life, and a man whose friendship it is pleasant to remember. So Professor Rich appears to me as I think back gratefully to the days when it was my privilege to know him. There is no stain on the memory he leaves behind him. He was a clean, good man.

GEORGE HERBERT STOCKBRIDGE.

Of all the jewels of God's crown Thomas Hill Rich must shine among those preëminent for clearness and purity.

GEORGIA DREW MERRILL.

May 14, 1896.

It is not the labor of love but the privilege of love to offer this brief tribute to the memory of Thomas Hill Rich. Even as I write, after the lapse of years, his unique and charming personality stands out before me, clear-cut as a cameo, and as strongly impressed upon the unfailing inner consciousness of an affectionate remembrance as natural objects are photographed upon the retina of the vision. It was not so much one single trait that drew men to him. It was rather a union of qualities of mind, heart, and soul, in harmonious blending, that elicited the profound respect of those that knew him most intimately. "Worthy to bear, without reproach, the grand old name of gentleman," he conferred upon the title additional grace by his most sincere and consistent Christian life. I shall never forget how hospitable and kind he was to me, a stranger, when I first assumed the pastorate of the High Street Congregational Church, Auburn. In the early spring, before the chill had passed from the air, even before the last belated snow-flakes had ceased to whiten the earth, I turned my face northward to the somewhat frigid welcome of the Pine Tree State. But in the heart of Professor Rich, and in the hearts of other friends in the parish, I found compensating warmth and shelter. My first evening in his home, how well I remember it! The beaming face at the door; the high, innate purity of soul shining through the fleshly raiment of his finely-chiseled features; the fire of crackling logs upon the hearth-stone, a musical explosive which served but to accentuate the gentle murmur of conversation on men and books and studies; the delightful sense of perfectly assured good-will and sympathy for the pilgrim about to meet the inevitable difficulties of a new and untried field; the dainty, restful chamber, with skillful, housewifely touches, where I slept at peace with all the world—how that evening comes back to me as a fragrant memory now that years of perplexity and struggle in the advocacy of unpopular causes are merged in the waters of a wider and maturer experience!

And what my honored friend was at the beginning he continued to be to the very end, a firm, loyal, and consistent supporter of his pastor. Trained in the older theology, perhaps conservative by nature, and yet open to fresh light and truth, it followed, of necessity, that my views of religious doctrine were not always the opinions cherished by Professor Rich. But I cannot recall that we ever clashed for a single moment on points of doctrine or that the widest dogmatic divergence ever threw the least shadow upon our friendship. Through all — whatever may have been his personal belief — his lofty sense of loyalty to the minister of his choice held his tongue from acrid criticism and maintained his heart in affectionate allegiance. More than this, he appeared intuitively to recognize the right of the pulpit to absolute freedom in the discussion of all living questions, although, personally, I think Professor Rich, with his singularly scholarly instinct, did not much care for the presentation of topics outside the range of purely Biblical questions. In the best sense of the phrase he was a specialist in scholarship, and the accuracy of his mental processes I have seldom found surpassed among students of my acquaintance. And yet, along with this quality, that shrinks from slovenly work even as a thorough musician shrinks from false notes in orchestral combinations,—along with this quality Professor Rich showed wonderful considerateness toward pupils of natural dulness and incapacity. I remember being present at a class-room exercise in Hebrew where one or two young men made sad work of the construction in translating from the Prophets. I could see that Professor Rich was greatly put out by the exhibition. Those who knew him well will recollect a peculiar wrinkling of the lines of the forehead, a certain "I don't like that at all" expression whenever he was disturbed or annoyed. At the time mentioned the wrinkle was fully in evidence. But his manner toward the offenders was the very epitome of courtesy. "Surely, Mr. X, you do not mean this!" "Wouldn't you say rather that the verb is made from the root Z?" "Doubtless you intend a paraphrase of the lines in place of a literal rendering!" And thus, with infinite pains and unfailing helpfulness toward his pupils, the product of his own perfect breeding, the instructor virtually carried them through the hour and unraveled with luminous insight the intricacies of that tongue of which he was so admirable a master.

I wish I might speak more at length of the personal characteristics of my friend whose attitude toward me, his pastor, was the very embodiment of that sweet fraternity which ought ever to signalize the relations between a minister and his flock. Were I asked to name, in a sentence, the chief element in his nature which appealed most strenuously to his friends, I should say it was his unvarying habit of speaking kind words and doing kind deeds. If Professor Rich had criticisms to propose—and he was by no means lacking in the critical faculty—they were presented in a form absolutely incapable of offending the most sensitive spirit, and supported by cogent if not always convincing reasons. Easier for him, by far, to praise judiciously than to blame captiously. Indeed, the very gentleness of his nature forbade that occasional harshness of which impulsive but royally endowed men are sometimes guilty. He cherished the spirit of Sir Henry Sidney's maxim, "A wound given by a word is harder to heal than a wound given by the sword." Nor was it a gentleness unveined by the more rugged quality of firmness. Beneath the calm, quiet exterior there lurked indomitable perseverance, and also a certain vise-like tenacity of will. I may illustrate by an example. When the Rev. A. P. Tinker died, who for ten years was pastor of the High Street Church, commemorative memorial services were held in the church. Professor Rich was one of the speakers. Either through embarrassment, for I believe he never conquered a certain nervous timidity when facing an audience, or from lapse of memory, the substance of his address eluded forms of expression. Yet there he stood, unwilling to give up, waiting through long pauses for words and facts that obstinately halted, and still maintaining his position on the platform until the major portion of what he had to utter found deliverance. What he *must* do he *would*, and I am of the opinion that fire and water could not keep this outwardly shy, unobtrusive man from the achievement of his deep-lying purpose.

Of his rank in technical scholarship others are more competent to speak. Professor Fisher of Yale once said to us in the class-room: "The first mark of a scholar is accuracy." With accuracy of method which would satisfy the most imperative requirements of scholarship Professor Rich joined that unflagging industry whose results are disclosed in the thoroughness with which he mastered the critical details of Old Testament language and literature. I believe that phenomenal thoroughness is the prime cause of his failure oftener to publish. He would bring no other oil than "beaten oil" into the illuminating processes of his printed work. What he was to Bates College, to the twin cities, to the intellectual life of the community in which he lived and toiled, to his wife, his friends, his colleagues in education, is reserved for other pens to describe. My privilege has been to write of Thomas Hill Rich as I knew him personally and intimately in the pastoral relation—a privilege but poorly embraced amid the hurry and distraction of last days of preparation for summer flight to the sea-shore. His life followed the peaceful tenor of the scholar's work and mission, and ripened and mellowed with gathering years. Death came, not as a shock but as a fruition, and in the "sounding labor-house vast, of Being," to employ Matthew Arnold's felicitous metaphor, his soul to-day doubtless finds the sphere of usefulness reserved for self-forgetful men and women whose earthly consummation is but an epoch in the infinite service of humanity.

FREDERICK STANLEY ROOT.

"Love is the Fulfillment of the Law."

Oh, not in vain we live, if lives are made,
By our life's living, purer, unafraid
Of right, attuned to brave, unselfish deeds,
And brought to love the Giver of all creeds.

The one our halting pen would honor, but shrinks back
From inability to move along the track
He ever traveled—lived—on heights not often trod—
The fresh, green hills before the throne of God.

. . . .

His love to parents, friends, students, and all
Who in his charmèd circle chanced to fall—
So close to God he lived that child-like trust
And winsome sweetness forth like fountains gushed
From all his words and deeds. While warmth, and light
And Poesy, and all things fair and bright,
From childhood kept him far from other men,
Whose lower levels knew not of his ken.

W. A. FURGUSSON.
May 14, 1896.

[From Class Reunion Report, June 21, 1893.]

In the gymnasium, Wednesday evening, June 21, at six o'clock, were gathered around the table, Eastman, Humphrey, S. F., Newcomb, Rich, Sewall, Smythe, Stevens, Dinsmore. Old fellows we all were, every one having passed the three-score limit; but now were boys again.

No one had much to relate of the past five

years' experience, life having moved on in the same line much as during the previous five years. Rich is Professor of Hebrew at Bates College Divinity School. No one appeared more likely to continue in health and vigor, and be among those who should meet at the fiftieth anniversary, than Rich; but it seems that he was to be the first to fall out from our remaining number. On the 6th of July, only fifteen days afterwards, he died suddenly in Lewiston. Thus ended a remarkably pure, earnest, and studious Christian life. He was in his seventy-first year. Dinsmore writes: "How much he enjoyed being there (at the reunion), and how well he seemed at the time; and yet, in two weeks, was called to leave his beautiful home on earth to Mansions above, passing away without a pain or groan—a beautiful translation—just as he had desired to leave this world."

He had filled the professorship at Lewiston twenty-one years, and was revered and greatly beloved by all his students and a large circle of friends. His gentle, self-sacrificing, and laborious student life we all remember, and the same characteristics remained with him to the end, and made his life fruitful in the welfare and happiness of others, and the attainment of scholarly honors to himself. He published four translations from the Hebrew, which established his reputation as a Hebrew scholar; and was busy the last day of his life in a revision of a version of Habakkuk, which he was to give as a Bible reading at the approaching meeting of the Chautauquan Assembly, at Fryeburg. He was also a frequent contributor of articles to biblical periodicals, and was a member of the American Oriental Society, the Genealogical Society of Maine, the Maine Historical Society, and the Society of Biblical Literature and Exegesis.

. . . . . .

The intense sacredness with which Professor Rich invested his work in translating the Bible shines out in every line he wrote. How naturally his large faith in God found expression in his reverent rendering of the Messianic Psalms. Perhaps the most remarkable feature of his gifts was their complete symmetry.

. . . . . .

One thread runs through all his life, and this is, his love for his fellow-men, and his never-ceasing endeavors to lead them to nobility of life.

From a College Mate.

. . . . . .

When I first met Mr. Rich I was impressed with his personality. What a remarkable face he had—a broad mouth, a closely-shaven chin, a broad, high forehead, arched with a heavy brow, and underneath, large, clear blue eyes, with an expression of consciousness of responsibility. . . . . .

[Found in the scrap-book of Professor Rich.]

Over the Silent Sea.

Over the Silent Sea
Dear ones awaiting me
On the fair shore beyond—in heaven's rest.
No failing footsteps there;
Life—one triumphant prayer—
Home of Love " over there "—
Home of the blest!

Over the Silent Sea
Dear ones are beck'ning me.
Oft in my dreams I hear songs of delight;
Sometimes the starry skies
Seem to my earth-born eyes
Opening to Paradise—
Through gateway bright.

—C. W. D. R.

April 3, 1893.

LESSONS IN WORDS.

As there are lessons in stones and shells, in trees and plants; so there are lessons in words; and the lessons in the latter are no less worthy of our study than the lessons in the former; for nature and language are both divine.

Words stand for ideas; and there is nothing which more than our ideas influences our actions; and in our actions day by day consists our practice.

Since words affect our practice, since they are a part of our practice, and may be so useful—a word spoken in season, how good it is!—since words have so much to do with our practice, a talk about certain of them may not be unpractical.

As character is a matter that deeply concerns us, that is of prime importance, let us take that word first, and seek for the idea that lies behind it. We shall find that this word comes from the Greek Χαρακτήρ—indeed it is the Greek word itself with English spelling. Χαρακτήρ signifies that which is stamped or engraven on anything—as the figures on coins and seals; and so we use character to

designate the qualities of a man impressed upon him by nature or habit.

Originally all the qualities of man must have been amiable and excellent; for God made man in his own likeness. This likeness, if now marred and defaced, is not obliterated; but is still capable of renovation. Each pure thought, each high resolve, each noble act, tends to the restoration of the divine lineaments; and repetition of such thought, such resolve, such act, makes those lineaments more manifest.

In the epistle to the Hebrews, Chapter 1 : 3, the Authorized Version says that Christ is the express image of God's person; but the Revision that Christ is the very image of His (*i.e.*, God's) substance, while in the margin the Revision has: "The impress of His substance." This last is truest to the original; for there we find this very word Χαρακτήρ. If then the image of God is impressed, engraven, charactered on Christ, and we copy and imitate Christ, we shall win back to ourselves the traits that marked man before he had fallen from his first estate.

It is written that God is kind to the unthankful and evil, and that in this we should be like Him. God is essentially kind; we are bidden to become so—to acquire this trait —so the New Testament teaches. It teaches, too, that this kindness is not one of word alone, but also of deed—a kindness that forgives, is serviceable, and serves; and becomes a servant for Christ's sake. Our word kind is of Anglo-Saxon origin, and only a contraction of *kinned;* which suggests that we should be kind to all, because we are akin to all—because all men are our kindred, and kinship justly claims kindness. Hamlet says of his uncle and step-father, that he is "a little more than kin, and less than kind," because, in marrying Hamlet's mother, he was somewhat more than a blood relation, and at the same time had shown himself unworthy of our race —our kind.

Formerly they resented kindnesses; for to resent is, literally, to feel back, that is, to recognize, to be sensible of. And should we not be as sensible of benefits as of injuries?

Formerly, too, they could retaliate kindnesses: for to retaliate is to render like for like; and so an author of the seventeenth century writes: "God takes what is done to others as done to Himself, and by promise obliges Himself to full retaliation."

We read that it is a very good, and a very pleasant thing for brethren, that is, kindred, to dwell together in unity. We can see that this should be so, for all agree that man is a social being—a being formed for society. For this reason we should be sociable, not standing aloof from our fellow-men, not taciturn and reserved; but approachable, and likewise worthy of association.

And here let me remind you that the terminations *able* and *ible*, which we borrow from the Latin, denote capability or worthiness.

So the word agreeable signifies a capability of agreeing or a readiness to agree; which signification it might be well to keep in mind if we desire to be agreeable; for if we forever set ourselves in opposition to what others do and say we are dis-agreeable, and cannot expect to be much sought after.

But a readiness to accord with the views of others, a responsiveness to what they propose, makes companionship easy and often delightful. There are, indeed, those ready to assent to everything we say. The German styles such persons, "*ja herren*," *i. e.*, "the yes men." Such persons are too agreeable to be so in the accepted sense of the word; for we need variety to spice our intercourse, and there is great profit in discussion that shakes apart, that sifts questions and gives to us the different sides.

With sociability and agreeableness, conversation is closely joined. Coming from the Latin, this word tells of turning round, of whirling round, of the revolution of the months, of repetition, of interchange and familiarity. Thus the word conversation could set forth man's life, which is a busy round, oft repeated, and closely associated with his fellows. But, as this round is sometimes well and sometimes ill performed, this word was therefore applied to one's conduct, to his behavior. Such is the sense of the word in King James's Bible. But now, as you know, the word conversation is limited to discourse, to the interchange of sentiments, to the giving and taking of the same mutually. Conversation, therefore, is a thing of continuity, not broken like mere talk, and, as the corresponding Greek term ἀναστροφή suggests, should have an upward turn, an improving tendency.

The ready flow of conversation is checked by the presumptuous man, who hastens to claim precedence—often won by modest waiting—who would take the highest seat before bidden to go up thither. The arrogant man still more retards conversation by constantly demanding that his importance shall be acknowledged. The insolent quite interrupts conversation by his unusual behavior, by his violation, his contempt of established rules, whereby he declares his bloated pride and unbridled passion. When we transgress laws established by God or by common consent of mankind, we enter the sphere of wrong; we have suffered ourselves to be twisted off, to be wrung off, from adherence to rectitude; we have acquired guilt, that is, we have allowed a tempter to guile us away from the sole right path.

He who habitually treads the right path is righteous,—rightwise, as our old authors used to say. As "otherwise" is other way, and "likewise" is like way, so "rightwise" is right way, and the righteous man is therefore the right way man—the man whose life is marked by rightwayness, or as we now say by righteousness. Righteousness refers especially to right relations with our fellow-men. The man in right relations with God, according to the originals of Scripture, is the one set apart for God's service— . . . . . . Greek ἅγιως; and later to express the joy of that service the consecrated person was also called the friend, the pious worshiper of God— . . . . Greek ὁσίως. The psalmist in Ps. 86:2 prays that he may be preserved, because he is a pious worshiper of God; and in Psalm 16:10 we might translate: "Thou wilt not suffer thy pious worshiper to see the pit." Such an one, walking with God, might well be expected to be right and blessed in every regard. With this thought, it may be, the Anglo-Saxon calls him a holy man, that is a whole man. It is in accord with this that

James speaks of the "entire man"—lacking in nothing. The Greek ὁλόκληροι of James was applied to the Jewish priests, who were to be entire in all their members. And now the Christian, who is a spiritual priest, should have no moral deformity, should lack no Godlike trait. But, as it is not enough that the body should be without blemish and defect, but should have some fulness of development; so James would have his brethren not only entire, but also perfect, finished, full-grown men.

We speak of the perfect gentleman, and of finished manners; and yet without any thought that in such case there can be no more refining. In this same limited sense we are often to understand the perfection that the Bible enjoins. It calls us to what is attainable—to character, finished, complete, well-rounded out. Yet the completest character will still admit of growth; for what is in no way defective can still receive augmentation. The perfect child Jesus grew in wisdom and stature, and in favor with God and man. Jesus had favor with God because he did the things pleasing in God's sight. His prayers had acceptance, were granted—"in that he feared," as we read in the Authorized Version, which has in the margin "for his piety," that is, "for his godly fear," which last the Revision gives. This fear is not the fear of terror, but of caution, modesty, reverence. The figure underlying its Greek original εὐλάβεια is that of one who lays hold of anything well, *i.e.*, carefully, so as not to break or injure it; of one who proceeds cautiously in his design, so as to avoid injury to himself or others. The rendering of this passage (Heb. 5 : 7) by the Revision brings it into harmony with Heb. 12 : 28, the only other passage where the noun εὐλάβεια occurs, which reads: "Let us have grace, that we may serve God with reverence and godly fear." Thus Christians are exhorted to have the same reverent regard to God's will that Christ had, shown in his words, "Thy will, not mine, be done," in his constant humbling of himself in comparison with the Father, and in his exalting of the Father in word and deed, of which Christ's life was full. Here we find the true idea of worship. It is to declare with the mouth and heart God's worth, to acknowledge that He is worthy to receive the glory and the honor and the power, and to submit ourselves to God's worthy rule. We may show regard to worth in man, and in a sense may worship him. This is recognized in the corresponding Greek and Hebrew terms. The Hebrew says that Joseph's brethren worshiped him when they were in Egypt to buy corn; and that the Amalekites worshiped David (2 Sam. 1 : 2), and the woman of Jekoa and Bathsheba did the same; and there were those who drew nigh to worship Absalom, and the princes of Judah worshiped King Joash; although in all these cases "did obeisance" stands in our translations. In doing obeisance, in worshiping, the Oriental bows his face to the ground, as much as to say, as we do in words: "Your most obedient servant."

Homage has relationship to the Latin *homo*, and in feudal times described the act of the feudal tenant, when on being invested with a fief he promised upon his knees, in presence of his new lord, fealty to him—promised to be his vassal, his hommage; that is, his man. We justly pay hommage to men of pre-eminent usefulness and virtue, and do well to profess fealty to their principles. We do hommage to the Supreme Being when we give him our reverence and our devout affection.

But to return to the thought of εὐλάβεια. God has committed to each of us a work which we are to undertake with carefulness and conduct with cautiousness, lest we make it a broken and a worthless thing. Simeon did this with the work committed to him, for Luke applies to him the adjective εὐλαβής, one in origin with the noun εὐλάβεια. This adjective is also given to the men dwelling at Jerusalem on the day of Pentecost; gathered there, as it reads, from every nation under Heaven. Their regard for God's service may have led them thither, but the fact of their being there is the rather mentioned to show that the wonders of Pentecost were witnessed by men of carefulness, of weight of character, and not to be deceived by false appearances. The same epithet, εὐλαβής, is applied to the men who dared to carry Stephen to burial and to make great lamentation over him,—probably not Christian brethren, but Jews, whose reverence for God and His commands made them abhor the bloody deed.

Having dwelt so long on the carefulness of godly fear, it will not be amiss to say that what is done in a hurry is not likely to be well done; for, according to its derivation, hurry is the feeling that plunderers have, both when they are plundering and when they flee.

Haste, like hurry, is eager to accomplish; but is without confusion and without trepidation. But while one may hasten to finish a worthy work, he can afford to give it time, to stay by it until it is well done. If it is a work of magnitude it is likely that hardships will have to be borne, rebuffs will have to be resisted, and difficulties will have to be overcome before the work is achieved. All this requires endurance, persistence, perseverance; and all these are implied in the Greek ὑπομενή, which is literally the biding under; whose thought is expressed in Shakespeare's

"poor wretches
That bide the pelting of the pitiless storm;"

and in Bunyan's man of stout heart, who cut his way through the armed men "to the stately palace, beautiful to behold." It was illustrated in the case of Job, upon whom came down so many evils, and whose bearing under them James describes by this very word, which we there find translated patience. Alford renders it endurance, perhaps with some gain. Such is the patience whose perfect work makes the finished and the entire character,—which we well know is not wrought out in a day.

The Latin *coquo* tells both of food prepared by fire and of fruit ripened by the sun. Prefixing the Latin particle *prae*, the compound should tell us of food too soon cooked, of fruit too soon ripened. This compound gives us our word precocious, the too soon matured, the too soon cooked; which class of things and men lack the excellence that time and patience bring.

From the Latin *patror* (signifying to suffer), the root of patience, we also get passive, which denotes that which is acted upon, as one who undergoes medical or surgical treatment. Such an one is called a patient. When the soul is acted upon it has passion, and when the soul gives way to the passion of anger, the strong man, armed no longer, keeps his palace, but a stronger than he has come in upon him and overcome him. The soul has for the time surrendered its better self. The passion of Christ was the suffering which He underwent in His trial, His crucifixion, and His death.

The men spoken of above, who were so careful to please God, might be called accurate men, that is, men doing all in accordance with care. The Latin *cura*, embraced in the word accurate, is essentially our word care, and figures largely in English. The fisherman, with certain care-taking, preserves, cures his fish. The physician, by careful use of remedies, restores to health, cures his patient. The clergyman directs his care to the spiritual needs of men, and his work is sometimes called the cure of souls; and therefore all clergymen were once called curates. The office of a curate is a curacy. The curious person is one full of care,—it may be about his apparel, and then he is one fastidious in that respect. Or it may be that he is curious in his demands upon others, and then he is exacting and hard to please. Or all his care may be directed to learning, and then he is inquisitive and given to research; but if all his care is exercised about the concerns of others, the curious man is a prying person, meddler in other men's matters. A curious thing is one upon which many cares have been bestowed,—as the rare painting, the rare piece of statuary, the choice embroidery, the elegant piece of furniture—all objects in art and nature which invite careful attention are curious things, and those who give such attention have curiosity, and the things that receive it are curiosities.

In one denomination clergymen are said to care for the souls in their cure or curacy; in another they labor for them in their charge. Charge, coming from the French *charger*, to load or lade, to lay a burden upon, is also found in many connections. We load a gun and it is charged; a business matter is put into one's hands and he is charged with it, though the burden may be very light. The loaded vessel has a cargo, a form of charge which comes to us from the Spanish; in which language both the loader of cannons and the loader of vessels is called a *cargador*. By imitation of this form, it may be that we get our word stevedor, *i.e.*, stow-vedor.

A large dish, such as once bore a monstrous burden to Herodias, was formerly called a charger; a name also given to the horse, that bears to battle the burden of a warrior's weight, as in Campbell's familiar stanza :

> "By torch and trumpet fast arrayed,
> Each horseman drew his battle blade;
> And fiercely every charger neighed
> To join the dreadful revelry."

When solemn instructions are given to one entering upon the pastor's work, these as it were are a burden, a charge, which he is to take up and bear. A like burden is put upon the people now to become his flock. When crime is imputed to one, he is charged with it. When we magnify one's foibles and peculiarities, and in a sort, overload him, and put an undue burden upon him, we caricature him—a form of the word charge, derived from the Italian.

The accurate men of Acts, who dared to bury Stephen, in spite of the infuriated mob, may after all not have been courageous men, men of heart, for that is the meaning of courage, which comes from the Latin *cor*, or rather from the French *cœur*. Richard cœur-de-lion, lion-hearted, received this epithet, because abundantly endowed with animal courage. Courage is constitutional. But noble souls, even if not courageous, still prompted by worthy motives, do daring deeds, and are brave. In our late war a man of dauntless nature jeered his friend who had turned pale in the battle.

The friend replied: "If you had been so frightened as I, you would have fled from the fight." The one had courage, the other had principle, which prevailed over fear, and made him do bravely. Great Heart did not quail before giant Grim and the lions; and bade Christiana and Mercy and Christiana's boys follow him, and they did so; "but," says Bunyan, "the women trembled, and the boys looked as if they would die."

The Bible does not say that Moses was courageous, but perhaps intimates that he was not so. But Moses had respect unto the recompense of reward, and endured as seeing Him, who is invisible; and so he was faithful in all God's house, in all the great work that God laid upon him.

Men of crooked ways, and unfaithful to trusts, are so because they do not realize God's presence. George Herbert says: "Do all things like a man—not sneakingly. Think that the king sees thee; for *his* King does."

Bravery is thought of in the word virtue, which comes from the Latin *vir*, a man; not only a human being, but a man, adorned with noble qualities. Certain plants are said to have virtue, because they have power to counteract disease. Virtue went forth from the person of Jesus, that is, power to heal. Applied to character, virtue is moral excellence, which can only be won, and kept, by valor, energy, and constancy. Virtue is ever in need of heavenly aid, for

"Unless above himself he can
Erect himself, how poor a thing is man!"

Sincerity belongs to moral excellence. Some have thought that the word sincere comes from the Latin words *sine cera*, which tell of honey without wax—pure honey. This derivation is not secure. But there is no doubt about εἰλικρινής, which sincere represents in Philippians 1:10. Σἰλικρινής is: sun-judged. It teaches us that as we take a fabric to the sunlight to prove its texture, so our truth, our inward life, should be able to bear the testing of the brightest day.

To virtue, to moral excellence, we may well add charity. This word comes from the Greek χάρις, which is one with the Latin *gratia*, from which we get our word grace. While χάρις gives us our word charity and often occurs in the New Testament, still it is never translated by charity. We do indeed find charity twenty times in the Authorized Version, but it stands for the Greek ἀναπή, which the Revision more fitly represents by love; for charity is rather the manifestation of love than love itself. When love seeks not its own, when it is kind, and confers benefits, it becomes charity. Charity favorably interprets the words and the deeds of others, and aids them in their distresses. Of course charity begins in our homes. But if it has a true fountain in our home, there will be sure to flow from it streams, that will gladden multitudes, besides our own. God's pitying love led him to give his only Son for the world's salvation, and there is seen his favor to our race, that merited no favor; his charity, so to speak, his grace, which the Bible everywhere proclaims.

One has grace of manner, when his manners please and are looked upon favorably. In the religious use of the word one has grace when he has the favor of God, which should be manifest by his words and acts. We cannot always "resist the indignities of age," and shall have at length to give up the freshness and sprightliness of youth; but still we may grow old gracefully; may still be rich in the favorable regards of those about us, if only we possess a disposition full of sweetness; which we shall best secure by growing in the grace, *i.e.*, the favor, of our Lord Jesus Christ.

In repeated passages of the Bible we read that God is merciful and gracious. If in these passages we might have read, "God is merciful and graceful," *i.e.*, full of mercy and full of grace, the passages would have been more symmetrical. Here at least we might have given to the termination *ful* all its force, for the originals are what are called intensitives, words laden with the meaning of their root word. The translators, having to give up "graceful" because of the lower verb, did well to take "gracious," for that means abundant in grace.

Thus our God is a God of all grace, and we His children should be full of all goodness. Attaining somewhat of such excellence, we might then deserve to be classed among the best of men, and so could be called classic, for only that which is of the first class is so styled.

Every man must stand somewhere among his fellows, and so has rank; but rank is only attributed to those who have eminent position. Goodness should, and often does, bring one to the front, and so should confer rank. At any rate the good are God's noblemen.

"Life is a business; not good cheer;
Ever in wars."

But business has its relaxations, and in warfare the soldier is not always in the conflict of battle. So at times we may be diverted from severer pursuits, may seek diversion; at intervals may seek entertainment; when we are weary and vigor is impaired and our powers are no longer fresh we do well to seek refreshing—to seek to be refreshed; and when there have been great drafts upon us and we are exhausted and, so to speak, worn out, we should seek recreation, that is, should seek to be re-created. But diversion, entertainment, refreshing, recreation, tell of earnest work already done, and presently to be resumed.

"Life is real and life is earnest,"

for in it there is much to be brought to a head or, more elegantly and using one word for four, there is much to be achieved. Who shall teach us how to bring all our works to a successful issue, how to be achieving? Often in the New Testament when Christ is called Master, the original has διδάσκαλος, which is properly teacher—school-master, it might be. The law was not school-master, as the Authorized Version says in Galatians 3:24, but rather was like the slave, who at Athens led the boy to school and was his tutor, *i.e.*, his guardian, on the way thither. So the Revision reads the law was our tutor to bring us to Christ. Christ the teacher bids us come to Him to learn. The Greek for learner is μαθητής, which in the New Testament is represented by disciple, which is, properly, a little learner, a diminutive, testifying of humility in the learner and of tender love on the part of the teacher. If as true disciples we come to learn of Christ the Teacher, He will show us the way to achievement, even the way to win a kingdom and life everlasting.

The Greek verb παρακαλέω is literally, to call to or by one's side, an then to exhort, as to battle, and to beautiful deeds. Παρακλητος a derivative of the verb just mentioned, designates one called to one's side for help, especially in a court of justice,—an advocate. The original has παρακλητος in the passage that says: "We have an advocate with the Father, Jesus Christ the righteous." Adopting this Greek word, with a slight change, we have our word Paraclete — applied to the Holy Spirit. His help, too, may be invoked, for He is ready to help our infirmities. We may give to παρακλητος an active sense, and then it represents the Holy Spirit as near by and calling us to battle with the sin within us and about us, exhorting us to the pursuit of all that is lovely and of good report.

Παράκλησις, exhortation, is likewise from παρακαλέω. It describes Barnabas, who was rather a son of exhortation than a son of consolation; and so we read a little further on in Acts 11, even in the Authorized Version, that when Barnabas came to Antioch, he exhorted them all with full purpose of heart to cleave unto the Lord. The exhorting of these words is not given in coldness, but is full of heart and cheer. We might render them severally by encourage, encourager, encouragement. This last is well placed by the Revision in Hebrews 6 : 18, for to those who lay hold of the Gospel hope the immutability of God's counsel is rather a source of strong encouragement than of strong consolation. The encouragement is broader and takes in consolation. And so we see that while the Holy Spirit exhorts to battle and to beautiful deeds, He cheers with promise of victory and of the exceeding great reward.

The transliteration paraclete is not found in the New Testament, but there The Comforter stands for ὑπαράκλητος, when used as a designation of the Holy Spirit. But comforter is from the Latin *confortare*, which, embodying in itself the Latin adjective *fortis*, is plainly to make strong, and only in a secondary sense, to console. In this, its primary sense, comfort is often met with in our early literature.

In Luke 1 : 80, where we now read : "And the child grew and waxed strong in spirit," Wyclif renders : "And the child waxed and was comforted." And later, Tyndale renders Luke 22 : 43 : "And there appeared an angel unto him from Heaven, comforting him," where we now read that an angel from Heaven strengthened Christ.

We need not only to be strengthened in our sorrows—consoled if you will, but to be strengthened in temptation and in all our work of life, that we may resist the evil and cleave to duty. We are compassed by infirmity, and every moment have need of help. But God is more willing to give the Holy Spirit to them that ask than parents are to give good gifts to their children; and the Holy Spirit is the Comforter.

> "Why, therefore, should we do ourselves this wrong,
>   Or others—that we are not alway strong—
> That we are ever overborne with care—
>   That we should ever weak or heartless be,
> Anxious or troubled—when with us is prayer,
>   And joy, and strength, and courage are with God?"

which come to us through the Holy Spirit, the Comforter.

Thus words tell us of work, of diligence in its performance, of help at hand, whereby we make it successful and victorious.

> "Life is real! Life is earnest!
>   And the grave is not its goal;
> Dust thou art, to dust returnest,
>   Was not spoken of the soul.
>
> "Not enjoyment, and not sorrow,
>   Is our destined end or way;
> But to act! that each to-morrow
>   Find us farther than to-day.
>
> "Lives of great men all remind us
>   We can make our lives sublime,
> And departing, leave behind us
>   Footprints on the sands of time;—

"Footprints, that perhaps another,
　　Sailing o'er life's solemn main,
　A forlorn and shipwrecked brother,
　　Seeing, shall take heart again.

"Let us then be up and doing,
　　With a heart for any fate;
　Still achieving, still pursuing,
　　Learn to labor and to wait."

January, 1887.

Copied and revised August 5, 1887.

T. H. RICH.

www.ingramcontent.com/pod-product-compliance
Lightning Source LLC
Chambersburg PA
CBHW021950160426
43195CB00011B/1299